Transportation

Airplanes

by Mari Schuh

CAPSTONE PRESS
a capstone imprint

Little Pebble is published by Capstone Press,
1710 Roe Crest Drive, North Mankato, Minnesota 56003
www.mycapstone.com

Library of Congress Cataloging-in-Publication Data
Library of Congress Cataloging-in-Publication data is available on the Library of Congress website.
ISBN: 978-1-5157-7305-4 (hardcover)
ISBN: 978-1-5157-7311-5 (paperback)
ISBN: 978-1-5157-7317-7 (eBook PDF)

Summary: Provides a general overview of airplanes, including their features and the different types of airplanes.

Editorial Credits
Carrie Braulick Sheely, editor; Lori Bye, designer; Wanda Winch, media researcher;
Katy LaVigne, production specialist

Photo Credits
Alamy Stock Photo: SCPhotos, 13; iStockphoto: santirf, 20 – 21; NASA: Kennedy Space Center Photo Archive, 19; Shutterstock: Action Sports Photography, 15, Marcel Derweduwen, 9, MP_P, 11, T. Sumaetho, zoom motion design, tratong, 6 – 7, VanderWolf Images, 16 – 17, Volodymyr Kyrylyuk, 5; U.S. Air Force photo by TSgt Ben Bloker, cover

Table of Contents

Up High

Look up in the sky!

An airplane flies high.

Parts

See the jet engines?

They are loud.

They make this airplane move.

jet engine

jet engine

A propeller spins fast.

It can move an airplane too.

See it go!

Airplanes have long wings.

They lift airplanes into the air.

Up they go!

Pilots fly an airplane.

They move levers.

They look at dials.

lever

Kinds

A crop duster flies low.

It is slow.

It sprays crops.

A fighter flies high.

It is fast.

It shoots at an enemy plane.

Cargo planes are full of goods.

They can carry mail too.

Some can carry cars.

A jumbo jet flies far.

It carries many people.

Where will you fly?

Glossary

cargo—the goods carried by an aircraft, ship, or other vehicle

crop—a plant farmers grow in large amounts, usually for food

dial—the face on a measuring instrument

enemy—one that tries to harm another

engine—a machine that makes the power needed to move something

fighter—a fast airplane with weapons that can destroy other aircraft

goods—things that can be bought or sold

lever—a bar or rod used to run a machine or vehicle

pilot—a person who flies a jet or plane

propeller—a set of rotating blades that make the force to move an airplane through the air

Read More

Adamson, Thomas K. *Airplanes.* Blastoff! Readers: Mighty Machines in Action. Minneapolis: Bellwether Media, 2017.

Peterson, Megan C. *The First Airplanes.* Famous Firsts. Mankato, Minn.: Capstone, 2015.

West, David. *Planes.* What's Inside? Mankato, Minn.: Smart Apple Media, 2017.

Internet Sites

Use FactHound to find Internet sites related to this book.

Visit *www.facthound.com*

Just type in 9781515773054 and go.

Check out projects, games and lots more at
www.capstonekids.com

Critical Thinking Questions

1. What parts of an airplane help it fly?

2. What do different kinds of airplanes have in common?

3. How can airplanes help people?

Index